the

WORKING MOTHER

ULTIMATE GUIDE

to

WORKING FROM HOME

HOW TO SURVIVE IN YOUR JOB, CARE FOR YOUR KIDS, AND STAY SANE

From the Editors of the No. I Destinatio ns

Skyhorse Publishing

Skyhorse Publishing books may be purchased in bulk at special discounts for sales promotion, corporate gifts, fund-raising, or educational purposes. Special editions can also be created to specifications. For details, contact the Special Sales Department, Skyhorse Publishing, 307 West 36th Street, 11th Floor, New York, NY 10018 or info@skyhorsepublishing.com.

Skyhorse® and Skyhorse Publishing® are registered trademarks of Skyhorse Publishing, Inc.®, a Delaware corporation.

Visit our website at www.skyhorsepublishing.com.

10 9 8 7 6 5 4 3 2 1

Library of Congress Cataloging-in-Publication Data is available on file.

Cover design by Brian Peterson
Interior images by Getty Images

ISBN: 978-1-5107-6593-1
Ebook ISBN: 978-1-5107-6594-8

Printed in the United States of America

CONTENTS

INTRODUCTION

It started, like most mortifying stories do, with a misunderstanding.

My husband and I were both working from home, and we were triple-booked at 1 p.m. I was being interviewed for a podcast. My husband, an attorney, was conferencing a case virtually. But our son's school was holding a virtual town hall. After a quick negotiation, we agreed my husband would listen to the school call.

Unbeknownst to me, he put on headphones and listened in from his cell phone, so he could still "attend" his work meeting from his laptop. I happily chatted with the host of the podcast, assured he was taking notes of anything we needed to know.

When I finished up the recording, my husband yanked the headphones out of his cell phone, and the principal's voice suddenly filled our living room. I was confused. Had my husband *just* joined the call? Panicked thoughts rushed through my head. *Did we miss vital information? Is the school being closed down and now we'll never know???*

"I thought you were LISTENING!" I shouted.

"I WAS listening! But I was WORKING too!"

"Well, what did they SAY?"

"I don't KNOW! They just keep talking about MASKS!"

Suddenly, my phone lit up with a text from a mom friend at the school. I read it. My heart stopped. "You aren't on mute!!"

WE. WEREN'T. ON. MUTE.

Frantically, I started signaling to my husband to mute the mic. He thought I was choking. "We aren't on mute!" I whispered.

"Yes, we are," he said, aloud, looking at his phone in confusion.

"The assistant principal had to mute you," my friend texted, after I assume she stopped laughing hysterically.

THE. ASSISTANT. PRINCIPAL. HAD. TO. MUTE. US.

That's right. I had an argument with my husband, captured live on Zoom, for the ENTIRE SCHOOL COMMUNITY to witness. Why, yes, I am dying of embarrassment. Your best wishes are appreciated.

Apparently, yanking the headphones out of the cell phone had somehow overridden the school's auto-muting.

I stared at my phone in horror. I texted another friend, "Did you hear us arguing?"

"I didn't know that was you! Haha!"

And then I realized I'd outed myself. Two moms now knew of my infamy, which meant the gossip would surely make the rounds of the entire PTA. We would forever be that couple who fought at the school town hall. Our fate was sealed.

Why, might you ask, am I sharing this moment with the world? Here at *Working Mother*, we are big believers that moms should be transparent about our struggles. For too long, women have quietly served as the backbones of our families, workplaces, and communities—and we have too little to show for it. At the very least, the world should have to hear from us.

And now the entire school has heard from me. I'm embarrassed, but I don't regret it. This is what it looks like to be a dual-income working family in 2020, struggling with the weight of a thousand obligations, all in one small space.

You might not have been caught having a mortifying meltdown in front of your school's parent body, but I'd bet you wrestled with one of the many challenges of working from home: keeping your kids entertained and learning. Minimizing a thousand interruptions and staying focused. Managing a calendar that's overloaded with Zoom calls. Preparing way too many snacks and lunches and putting away a never-ending pile of dishes and laundry.

If you're partnered, you've probably struggled to split the load equally with your spouse. If you're single, the workload likely seems overwhelming.

We're here to help. For more than forty years, *Working Mother* has served as a mentor, role model, and advocate for working parents. Even before the COVID-19 pandemic upended the way we all work and live, we advocated for remote work and flexible schedules, because we know these policies help working parents come a step closer to achieving some semblance of work-life balance.

That's crucial. Parents with access to perks like remote work and flexible schedules are far less likely to quit, and they report higher levels of job satisfaction and productivity. In a time when moms are leaving the workforce in startlingly high numbers—a development that threatens to set women's progress back by a generation—remote work might be one of the best ways to reverse this troubling trend.

That's because, despite its challenges, working from home can be a pretty sweet setup for parents.

Last year I watched my baby girl learn to crawl and take her first steps—milestones I missed with her older brother, because I was busy working in an office all day. I can now talk to my kids' pediatrician without sneaking off to an empty conference room to avoid bothering my coworkers. I can take a more active role in my son's education, because I know what he's learning every single day. I no longer spend hours each week commuting to and from my office (and frantically worrying about paying those dreaded daycare overtime fees when traffic is untenable). I take a quick jog at lunchtime, and I don't have to worry if I'm sweaty when I get back. I wear yoga pants. Every day.

Here at *Working Mother*, we've decided to embrace this new remote work world permanently, and we're not alone. A McKinsey analysis suggests that more than 20 percent of the workforce could work remotely three to five days a week as effectively as they could working from an office. Companies like Facebook and Microsoft have already announced that a big chunk of their workers can clock in remotely going forward, and it's a safe bet more will follow.

If you're one of the parents who plans to work from home from now on, or if you've already been reaping the benefits of remote work—but struggling to stay productive—we hope this book will serve as a useful guide. It's a compilation of *Working Mother*'s best articles on the topic—chock-full of helpful hacks, smart tools, and the validation you need to get it all done without losing your mind. You are not alone. We're all in this together.

You'll find plenty here on mitigating the woes that come with working from home: establishing boundaries between work and family, fighting fatigue and burnout, setting a schedule and sticking to it, cutting down on distractions, staying motivated, and more.

No matter if you're aiming for the executive ranks or just want to bring in some extra income for your family, you deserve the peace of mind that comes with doing your best as a parent and employee. We hope you find it here.

And never forget: Mute your mic.

Keep climbing,

Audrey Goodson Kingo
Editor in Chief

HOW TO WORK FROM HOME WITH A BABY

An executive VP shares her tips for balancing work and raising her infant amid a global crisis.
by Lianne Wiker Hedditch

Being a new mom is an amazing challenge in and of itself. Since having my son nine months ago, I have experienced the high of a love like none other, the low of postpartum depression and every emotion in between. Once my maternity leave was over, and I got into the rhythm of working again and feeling comfortable and confident in his daycare, bam—here comes a pandemic.

Working with a newborn at home is definitely difficult. My son is not old enough to e-learn and requires attention from the moment he wakes up until he goes to sleep. Today I'm sharing a few tips on how my husband and I have found a working balance to keep everything moving.

1. Set a routine for yourself.
While it's too soon to really get your infant on a structured timeline, if you are type A like I am, you will need a structure for yourself. Still set an alarm and shower before your little one wakes up. Take

a few hours of normalcy after your child's bedtime to vent with your girlfriends or enjoy a glass of wine.

2. Create a shared calendar with your significant other.
With a baby that cannot communicate its needs, it is so important that someone is always available. My husband and I have gotten into the routine of adding our meetings to each other's Google calendars so that we are sure that, as much as possible, we are not overlapping in other priorities at any time.

3. Find new toys that entertain and are great for development at your infant's age, introducing something new each week.
Our current favorites are the Skip Hop 3-Stage Activity Center, the Joovy Spoon Walker, the Fisher-Price Learning Cube and Laugh & Learn Smart Stages Puppy and anything from Kido here in Chicago!

4. Expand the feedings and nighttime routine.
My daycare sends photos of my infant making works of art, learning music with live guitar lessons and doing yoga. And as the saying goes, "Ain't nobody got time for that!" I still find time for developmental lessons in the day-to-day, practicing pincer grasp during lunch, holding the bottle in the evening and more. Spend a little extra time together at each feeding break, and at night, read a few extra books and sing a few more songs.

5. Set out a balanced meal plan, even for an infant.
Do this if your child has started solids, to take care of what daycare traditionally provides. Make sure that they are exploring new textures and flavors.

6. On the weekends, turn "family time" into "personal time."
We are all in an abundance of the former right now. Where you usually would carve out activities with the kids, get some alone-time

R&R. Take that bubble bath, make that phone call and let your significant other handle your little one.

Above all, remember, this is cherished time that you won't get back.

I feel lucky that I've been home for my son's first words ("dada"—sigh), and for him to learn how to crawl—two things that otherwise he would have been at daycare for.

Keep Babies and Toddlers Occupied

Older kids are often happy to play video games for hours, but it's harder to keep babies and toddlers from interrupting your work every 10 minutes. Here are some great ways to keep them focused on having fun without Mommy:

1. Hide toys and reintroduce them one at a time to get your child excited about playing with them.
2. Walk around your home with your child as you take calls. Kids crave frequent changes of scenery.
3. For older toddlers (who are past the stage of tasting *everything*), fill a water table with interesting textures.
4. Repurpose household items into art supplies. They make more interesting canvases for drawings and sticker scenes than plain paper.
5. Encourage scavenger hunts by hiding toys around the house, and let kids raid cabinets without sharp, fragile items.

WORKING FROM HOME MEANS NOT HAVING ANOTHER PLACE TO MENTALLY LEAVE YOUR JOB BEHIND

Longtime-remote moms and mental-health experts share how to separate work and family, even when they're occupying the same space.

by Angela Repke

I was working from home long before the coronavirus outbreak, and it definitely had its perks. If the kids were sick, I was able to care for them without scrambling to find childcare. Plus, I could throw in a load of laundry whenever I needed. But the hardest part about working from home in that pre-pandemic world was that I didn't have a place to leave my work mentally. And it's a new struggle for those of you joining the fully remote ranks.

When you physically go to a workplace, it's much more feasible to leave your work there—it'll be there tomorrow. But when you're always at home, your brain is clogged with ideas and things you need to focus on, even after business hours. Your mind never rests—which makes it increasingly difficult to concentrate and be present with your family. But what can we do about it?

One action that we can take is to set time parameters. A practice that Christine Moffatt, a mom in the marketing business, implements is to make sure her work is done by the time the weekends roll around—"especially Sundays." It's important to stick to the same

Monday through Friday schedule as if we *did* work in an office. This way, our minds will be able to shift to "weekend time" with our families.

Christine also implements a rule where she doesn't work from her bed. She said, "It was the worst habit for me. Nothing like getting out of bed with a head full of anxiety!" I can attest to this one too. Technology is a valuable tool, but we can't escape it. I check my email hourly. It doesn't matter if the kids are around or not. So turning off technology until normal working hours is essential to mentally leaving work at a distance—even if it's not physically elsewhere.

After speaking with many women, the biggest obstacle is not having a separate workspace. Yes, you can create one in your home, but it doesn't mean that you won't be staring at the scattered Legos right beside your feet. Writer Lisa Davis said, "I'm sitting here working amid the mess, distracted by it." If your home is cluttered, your brain is too. It's difficult for me to work if I can see something that needs to be picked up, swept or wiped. It's like my brain can't move forward until my workspace is entirely clean. Luckily, there are ways to remedy this.

"It's vital to create a separate, and at the very least, consistent, workspace," says Julie Kays, manager and clinical counselor at the Counseling Center at Stella Maris in Maryland. Even if you can't have a separate room to mimic an office, sit at the same table and chair every single day—so that mentally, it becomes your work area. Be sure the surrounding area is clean the night before so that you can get right to work when business hours begin the next day.

Following strict times to change your clothes is another way to help your mental shift when you don't go to an office. Author Julie Lieberman Neale said, "For some time, inspired by Mr. Rogers, I was working to physically change something on my body, like changing clothes or putting on slipper socks, to acknowledge the transition of the day." When work time is over, something must be done to help your brain get the signal that it's not time to work anymore—it's now time for family. With a wardrobe change, you're not physically leaving laptops and files at a workplace, but your mind can shift to unwinding time.

Not only do we owe it to our families to leave work aside during after-hours, but we owe it to ourselves too. Our mental health can't be jeopardized, especially not at a time like this. With work constantly swirling in our minds because we don't exit an office, we're not giving ourselves a fighting chance. Find out how and where you get the most work done when you're on the work clock. Then you'll have a clear mind when it's time to share this same workspace with the ones you love most.

Minimize Work Distractions When You're with Your Kids

Just as our work deserves our undivided attention, so do our kids. Keep the focus on family time with these tips:

1. Talk openly with your colleagues about good and bad times of day for calls. Request ample advance notice for calls.
2. Block your own calendar when you have family commitments, plus block 5 to 10 minutes before and after meetings to provide necessary buffers.
3. Communicate your schedule. It's OK to not work full regular business hours every day, but you have to ask for what you need and let others know when you're available.
4. Turn off your phone's notifications when you're with your children. Give your coworkers one way you can be reached in case of an emergency—by text, for example—and then try to ignore your phone.

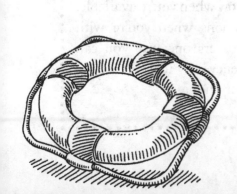

DON'T FEEL GUILTY FOR NOT GIVING YOUR ALL TO YOUR KIDS RIGHT NOW. WE'RE IN SURVIVAL MODE

Being the perfect parent, perfect worker and perfect human is just not possible in this moment.

by Mita Mallick, Diversity & Inclusion Thought Leader

Apparently it was St. Patrick's Day.

Because I was no longer physically in the office, there was no colleague I saw dressed in a green leprechaun T-shirt. Because I continue to be personally responsible, there was no happy hour where I could go sip a fun green cocktail. Because most of Jersey City is shut down, there was no parade to remind me either.

Then there were all of the preschoolers. They were quick to remind me.

All of the preschoolers. With their pictures posted in their "learning from home" designated areas on the school app and the Whatsapp and featured in text exchanges. Dressed in green. Some head to toe, others just a sprinkling. Green hair accessories. Green socks. Green shirts. And one, with a green hat. Their moms clearly didn't have a #momfail moment.

Happy St. Patrick's Day indeed. Now I was in search of a green cocktail. Or any cocktail would do.

"Mommy, can we check the app today?" my 4-year-old asked.

"Oh, honey, it's down today," I said, putting my phone away. "See, not working, app not working," as I shook my phone up and down and all around. Then distracting her with the next homework assignment we had to undertake.

Other than a cucumber, and a few unripe bananas, we owned nothing green for the moment. This would not end well.

In the COVID-19 era, so many of us working mothers are under pressure. Schools and teachers are doing their jobs, sending thorough lessons each day to be completed. Parents are sending along extra links to arts and crafts, additional worksheets, and ideas for exercising, including freeze dance, kids' yoga poses and meditation. All with the best of intentions.

Except the reality is I have to work. My husband and I both have to work from home. And I don't have time to teach my 4-year-old and 7-year-old. I don't have time to complete all the assignments, share pics on apps, send additional ideas, and then do it all over again. If I can get them out of their pajamas with their brushed teeth and sitting and eating breakfast quietly while we scramble to do a chunk of emails, well that's a big win for the day.

And so I don't know if my kids are learning. In fact they might unlearn how to read *Sam I Am,* unlearn how to hold a pencil, unlearn to sip out of a cup, unlearn how to count, to spell their own names, and God forbid unlearn how to use the bathroom on their own.

Here's what I do know:

I can't force them to do every assignment that was assigned for that day. If they skip an assignment that's OK. If they only complete one, that works too. I tried to get my preschooler to finish the last three questions on the worksheet before we started lunch and that exploded into a 15-minute tantrum.

I can't expect that their school schedule translates perfectly into a "learn from home" schedule. Because it doesn't. Circle time with stuffed animals doesn't work; naptime has disappeared; life skills means they watch another hour of Netflix and don't clean up the stuffed animals that got kicked around during failed circle time. They aren't in school with their friends and teachers; their normal has disappeared and they, like we, are in search of a new normal.

I can't feel guilty for not participating in St. Patrick's Day, crazy sock day, yellow day, animal day, mismatched day or (insert commercial made-up holiday here). I just can't. It was a win when we participated in crazy sock day when they actually went to school. All bets are off while "learning from home." And a picture to share? Not happening. Can I suggest a pajama day? Because that might work. With my luck, my kids will change out of their pajamas on pajama day.

Here's what I do know. My husband and I will continue to take shifts during the day. We will read to them; we will make silly faces and talk in funny voices. We will draw some animals and some ice cream cones too. We will make lunch together. We will watch Netflix together. We will wrestle on the floor. We will go for a fake nature walk in the city (more than once). We will watch more Netflix. We will read again. We will cuddle. We will say good night. Then my husband and I will drink and work to cope with the madness. And start all over again. Until this madness ends.

So I won't feel guilty for not teaching my kids while I have to work. I am in survival mode right now. We all are.

And if my 4-year-old has to repeat preschool, it's going to be OK. And in the meantime, I'll find a leprechaun shirt on clearance and stash it away. There's always next year.

Nonscreen Activities for Kids at Home

Even in the most desperate of days, we know we can't just leave Netflix running for hours (well, at least not *every* day we're working from home with kids). Once they get bored of all the toys they finally have tons of time to play with, try these other options that don't involve much effort on your part:

1. Fill a clear zip-top bag with paint, sand, or any flour or nontoxic powder that doesn't stick together. Have your child trace their finger over the bag to create designs inside. Mess-free (as long as that bag stays closed)!

2. Have the kids roll up newspaper or catalog pages into individual balls. Then, they should take turns pitching them into different receptacles—shoeboxes, mixing bowls, suitcases—from different distances and different positions, say, over their heads, between their legs, upside-down, and lying down.

3. Coloring books only hold attention for so long. Whip out other media, such as cardboard boxes, paper towel rolls, paper bags, paper plates, and coffee filters, and suddenly it's a whole new activity. Give them some special art supplies for decorating their canvases: yes, crayons, markers, and watercolors, but also stickers, pompoms, beads, and the glue they'll need to affix them.

4. Save some boxes for fort building! Have your child gather those as well as the typical fort materials—blankets, pillows, and chairs—and set up camp. Give them books and a flashlight so they can "read" inside their safe space.

5. Speaking of blankets and pillows, corral all of them into a single spot on a carpeted (or rug-covered) floor in your home, away from furniture and walls. Encourage your kids to jump into them . . . over and over. They can do belly flops, cannonballs, or even forward rolls. Helmets and knee pads are welcome.

6. Dump out your plastic bowls, strainers, ice cube trays, spoons, and spatulas and encourage your kid to stack, sort, and even bang (if you can still work through the noise). If you're a master of concentration, break out the metal pots and pans too.

7. Got some old magazines lying around? We give your kids permission to cut them up with safety scissors and glue their favorite pictures onto construction paper. For older kids, give them a list of items to find in each issue and cut out.

8. If you have a long hallway, create an "obstacle course" using pillows, chairs, stools, or whatever you can round up. This works especially well if you have more than one kid—they can compete to see who can finish the course faster.

9. Make a list—with simple drawings for the not-yet-reading folks—of items in your home that your child should go hunting for. That should buy you at least half an hour.

10. Put Alexa or Google Home to use: Your child can ask them to tell jokes, stories, and more.

11. Fill zip-top bags with uncooked beans, rice, or sand for little kids to squish.

12. If you're lucky enough to have bubble wrap on hand, tape some to the floor and tell your kids to jump around until every last bubble has popped. Not recommended for use during conference calls.

13. Round up all the balls (pun intended) and have your kids roll them toward different (unbreakable) things to knock down—empty cereal boxes, water bottles, and the like. When bowling gets old, tell your children to race two balls at a time toward a wall or door; keep

having the balls compete to see which one is the fastest. Encourage them to crown a winner and create a congratulatory card for the triumphant ball.

14. Some dry-erase markers work on windows. Test to see if yours can serve as a canvas—and, more importantly, if a rag wipes away the color. If so, let your kids go to town on the windows and show you their creations during a call you don't need to contribute to. Then, time them to see how quickly they can make all their artwork disappear.

15. No coloring books at home? Create one for free at **https://hoorayheroes.com/stories/freebies/**, and customize the character to look like your child. When you're done, the site will email you a PDF of the pages for printing.

ARE WORKING MOMS BETTER OFF WITH REMOTE OR ON-SITE JOBS? I'VE DONE BOTH

The right working environment for one mom isn't right for another.
by Laurie Cutts, Head of Partnerships & Media,
Acceleration Partners

In almost half of all two-parent households, both parents are full-time employees, according to Pew Research Center. Fortunately, more workplaces are offering greater flexibility to employees to balance the demands of a career with parenthood.

Working remotely allows many mothers to excel in both respects, but making the choice between working in an office or from home relies on different factors for everyone. Remote workers can struggle with distractions and a lack of socialization and collaboration at home, and working mothers have even more to factor into the equation.

I'm familiar with the advantages and disadvantages of working both on-site and remotely. If you're deciding whether to go into the office or set up a home office, here are a few things you should consider.

Staying On-Site
I've done the juggling act familiar to so many working mothers:

wanting to deliver great results at work while ensuring that my kids are getting the care they need.

Previously, I felt energized working in the office, with its innovative environment. Working on-site got me out and around other adults, including peers who wanted to pursue meaningful work and build a family.

The open-office environment was great for learning and communicating, but it could also be distracting with nonstop phone calls, meetings and noise within the shared space. With limited time in my day, I was very focused on output. Moreover, a 2.5-hour commute meant less time for my kids.

Going Remote

I now work from home, which allows me to pursue meaningful work and still invest in my private life. This has made a big difference in terms of my professional satisfaction and personal happiness.

Being home allows me to participate more holistically in my children's lives. It's much easier to get to special events at school, manage schedules, make dinner and check homework—things that strengthen a mother's relationship with her children. Not being constricted by a 9-to-5 schedule also opens up different childcare options, like a home daycare provider who has a shorter day.

Staying home has improved my work, too, as the time I spent commuting is now devoted to working. I typically feel more focused at home, especially when doing creative and thoughtful work. I can get into the flow more quickly.

Nonetheless, it can be hard to separate work from home. I sometimes struggle to tear myself away, and my kids wonder why I'm always in front of my computer. It goes without saying that children can also be distracting during work hours.

What's Right for You?

In my experience, the best solution is to strike a balance. I've done so by working remotely and going into the office once a week to connect with colleagues.

If your workplace gives you the freedom to choose where you work, the following questions can help you figure out your own balance.

1. Do you have a good space available for a home office?

You need a dedicated workspace that's separate from your family's living space. If my office door is closed, the kids know I'm working. When it's open, they're free to come in.

Having a designated office space not only keeps you focused on work, but it also helps you disconnect at the end of the day. Just as you can close the door on distractions while you're "at work," you can also close the door on work when you're ready to disengage.

2. Will you be distracted working from home?

You have to consider ways to work around distractions. Even with a private home office, shutting the door didn't always keep my young kids from interrupting.

They've been at daycare or in after-school programs while I've worked at home. If finding outside help isn't an option, try carefully scheduling your office hours to make the most of naptime.

3. Will you feel isolated?

Working remotely can be lonely. You don't have the same opportunities to socialize that you would in an office.

Even connecting with other work-at-home moms (who may follow different schedules) can be a challenge. If socialization and getting out of the house are high on your priority list, working on-site might be better.

4. Which is more cost-effective?

There are certainly financial benefits to working from home.

Primarily, it eliminates the cost of commuting, and you'll likely spend less on childcare.

With the cost of raising a child sitting at nearly $13,000 annually, working mothers could use the financial help. Remote workers also cut out wardrobe and meal costs. With additional tax breaks for having a home office, the average savings of working from home equal at least $4,668 a year.

5. Will you be happy and productive working from home?
Having more time with my kids while doing a job I love has made me happier tenfold.

This should really be your main consideration. Although remote workers consistently rate their happiness at work higher than the average score, you must determine what will make you happy.

Working remotely has helped me feel more successful as both a mother and a professional, but every woman has a different definition of balance.

The answers to these questions should help you align your priorities.

There's No Wrong Answer
Working mothers can have fulfilling careers and be successful moms at the same time. It's not easy, but it can be done. Weigh the benefits of working remotely in terms of cost and time savings against the potential for distractions and missed social opportunities to make your choice.

If you're pursuing satisfying work that you're passionate about, you're already setting a great example for your children—regardless of whether you work at home or in the office.

WORKING MOMS: HOW TO MANAGE A REMOTE TEAM AND A HOUSEHOLD

You need a specific plan so you can function well
for both your staff and your family.
by Cathy Sharick

A few years ago, I traded in my high-paced online journalism job, where I managed a team of fifty people around the world from my New York office, for a job managing three direct reports across the U.S. from the home office in my attic. I gave up the perks that come with a corporate office—IT departments, a bigger team to get tasks done, designer clothes and fancy coffee machines. Now, my commute time is measured in the seconds it takes to climb the third-floor stairs, my office attire consists of athleisure brands and pony tails, and I'm able to integrate my family into my daily work routine.

But difficulties can arise if you don't have a plan to manage your household while you manage your work. How can you stay productive at home while keeping track of your house and your family? It took me a while to figure out a system; it's not always perfect, but it works most of the time! Here are my four tips to keep your life sane and organized when you are working at home.

23

Create a Separate Workspace—and a Playspace
FOR WORK

For a while my new home office was wherever my laptop was: on the kitchen island, in the sunroom, on the back deck and sometimes even in my bed. With three little kids, this set up seemed amazing (at first). I was nearby when my toddler was eating lunch. I could work on projects while my second grader was coming home from the bus. I could listen in on my 5-year-old's conversations during her playdates. But I quickly realized that this lack of personal space led to chaos. I needed a place to work and to shut the door. I've now converted a small storage closet on the third floor of my house into my office. I'm able to shut off my family and concentrate when I need to get my work done. I invested in a good desk, office chair and lighting. My space helps me stay productive—and keeps out my family when I need quiet.

FOR HOME

I feel it's important to let my children see me working from time to time. For that reason, I set up a corner of my home office with a kids table and chairs where my little ones can sometimes come and color and draw or do homework during the week. My babysitter knows she needs to ask me before they come in. I've shared offices before, but can tell you that my three kids are my favorite office-mates ever—especially when they work quietly behind me (which does not always happen!).

Hire Incredible People
FOR HOME

It always shocks me when people ask if I have a babysitter now that I work from home. Um, yes. I have three kids! When you're working from home, it is essential to have the most reliable childcare possible. You need to be able to shut your door and work and know that your kids are well taken care of. My babysitter is the reason I'm able to do what I do, and without her, my household would fall apart. And luckily she is good with braids and bows.

FOR WORK

Hiring the right people for a remote team is crucial for your company's success. Not everyone is cut out for remote work, and not everyone really wants to do it. It's important to find people who are truly self starters and can work independently. You can usually tell if a person is independent through the interview process. If the candidate needs a lot of handholding during the interview, she or he is probably not right for the job. And all remote workers need to be great communicators. I make sure to check in with my direct reports a few times a day—and sometimes even a few times an hour—over Slack, Skype and email. I encourage people to ask questions. When you're working remotely, no question is ever a bad question. It's better to ask something that might sound silly than to keep going down the wrong path in the dark.

Make Plans and Do Your Best to Stick to Them

AT WORK

I have my team start every day by writing out their daily to-do's. We type our tasks into a shared scrum document (we use Google Docs) and start each day with a stand-up call over Skype. Each team member talks through his or her tasks for the day, and we share what we have accomplished the day before. I like to remind my staff that it's better to keep the list short each day—as short as possible when you're working at a high-intensity startup. Getting five to seven things done well is better than overwhelming yourself with too many tasks that will be done poorly.

AT HOME

I am not an amazing cook. I actually don't really like making dinner very much. But I do know that I like it when my family has a pretty healthy meal each night, and to have that happen I need to make a plan. I try to think through our meal plans on Sunday night and shop on Sunday or Monday. I set up a similar shared schedule for my kid's activities. Our shared family calendar hangs on the wall in my kitchen. If my husband or sitter or I don't write down an activity on this calendar, it's probably not going to happen.

Forget What You Think "Perfect" Looks Like
AT HOME
Don't try to be Pinterest perfect, and try not to fret over your high school classmate's idyllic status updates. It's not real life, but more importantly, it's not your life. Your house is never going to be that organized or that pretty, so why kill yourself over it? Instead, I like to focus on the impact I've made in my kids' lives, memories we've made, lessons they've learned, jokes we've shared. To me, that means more than a perfectly made bed ever will.

AT WORK
Remote work is not 9 to 5. You may have received gold stars at your office job by sitting at your desk for eight hours straight, but to achieve success while working on a distributed team, especially if you're working across time zones, it's imperative that you focus on productivity, not hours spent working. That means being able to show progress and goals achieved on a regular basis. No one is watching vigilantly to see if you take a lunch break or leave early to pick up your kids and then log back on after supper. But your team will notice if you miss a deadline or fall short on your promises. Get your work done but forget what your workday looked like when you were glued to an office chair in your in-house job.

4 WAYS TO MAKE THE MOST OF FAMILY TIME WHEN YOU WORK FROM HOME

The transition from cubicle to home office can be tricky.
Here are tips for maximizing flexible work.
by Marie Elizabeth Oliver

As the mother of a 1-year-old, I often get asked, "So, do you work, or stay home with your daughter?" To which I reply, "Actually, I have the best of both worlds. I work from home." As the managing editor of global startup PowerToFly, I work remotely, with a commute that lasts about as long as it takes me to walk down the hall. The benefits to this setup are obvious—I get to have lunch with my daughter and take advantage of the time I would otherwise spend getting ready and sitting in traffic to read and play outside with her.

But the transition from the cubicle to the home office isn't without its own speed bumps. When the physical division of your work and home life suddenly disappears, it's easy to lose sight of the fact that the point of a flexible job arrangement is to integrate the two in a way that benefits you. For me, it took careful planning, a move and some wise advice from colleagues to keep my "best of both worlds" situation from turning into the "worst of both worlds." Here's what I learned about maximizing family time in my first year working from home—and being a mother.

1. Be Upfront about What You Need

Think about what will make working from home work, whether it's transitioning your childcare setup (no, not even superwoman can work while watching a toddler) or creating a schedule outside the 9-to-5. Otherwise, you'll become too burnt out to enjoy any extra family time. "I'd advise other women who are transitioning back to work after a new baby (especially your first) to ask your employer for what you want, and be firm about what you need," says Jade Harris, a project manager who works remotely for RebelMouse. "You may be surprised at how much can be accommodated with a little creativity."

2. Stick to a Schedule

Book family time alongside your touch-bases and brainstorms. It's not uncommon for our shared calendars at work to include dance lessons and school pickup. Making a "reservation" holds you accountable and gives colleagues a heads up on where you'll be so you don't have to worry about checking your cell phone every five minutes. "I set a scheduled time with each of my kids a few times a month," says Cathy Sharick, our executive editor. "I take my toddler to her soccer class on Friday, I pick my son up from the bus twice a week, and I make sure to drive my daughter to school every day. Even scheduling in the small things with your kids matters."

3. Create a Functional Workspace

This was a lesson I learned the hard way. A dedicated workspace (read: not the dining room table or your bed) is essential to separating work time from family time. If your computer is out and open, you'll constantly be distracted when you're trying to spend time with your kids. Whether it's a guest room or a converted closet, a separate workspace is crucial to your success. "You need to define clear boundaries," says Lata Sadhwani, an iOS developer with 29th Street Publishing. "If possible, have it where you can be alone and can think without any disturbance."

4. Look for Creative Opportunities to Integrate

I have lunch with my daughter almost every day, and it's one of my favorite parts of working from home. Whether it's eating, working out or turning personal errands into an exciting adventure (I recently introduced her to the joys of shoe shopping), try out creative ways to use your non-work time to bond with your child. Nada Mihovilovic, one of my colleagues in Belgrade, Serbia, even transitioned her social happy hours: "A couple of years ago we were meeting in coffee shops. Now we arrange that time as playdates for our kids." A win-win!

ORGANIZE YOUR HOME OFFICE

If you feel like the organizing bug has bitten you, you are not alone.
Let us help you get your home office in order with these tips.
by Diane Albright, Certified Professional Organizer and
Productivity Consultant

If you are like most working moms, having more time likely tops your list of goals for this year. Creating an efficient organization system will allow you to obtain your goal. A Brother International Corporation survey revealed that an estimated 76 working hours per person each year are lost as a result of disorganization in the workplace. That amounts to almost two full weeks of unproductive time spent searching for lost work supplies, work papers and/or computer files. Proper organization is key if you are looking to save time in the new year.

Not only will disorganization rob you of productivity, it may send your boss, co-workers or clients the wrong message. The same study found that 71% felt that a cluttered desk is a sign of "a cluttered mind." The good news is that organizing your home office and gaining control over your time can be accomplished by following a few easy steps.

Tips for Home Office Organization

1. Have a designated place for everything. How many times have you found yourself looking high and low for a paper, directions or keys, and stressing out because you are running late for a meeting or appointment? The average American, in his or her daily life, wastes 55 minutes a day looking for items he or she knows he or she has but simply can't find. Placing your supplies in a designated location will enable you to locate them quickly and easily.

2. Purge. Get rid of what you don't need and don't want. If you haven't used an item in the past six months and don't know when you will use it next, then donate it. If it doesn't work, or is in disrepair, toss it or recycle it appropriately! Once you have finished purging, you can focus on what you have left.

3. Maximize your storage space by going vertical. Things you use regularly need to be close at hand. Things used less often can be stored up high or down low. Shelves, wall baskets, wall-mounted or magnetic file holders and hooks will be most helpful.

4. Select a label maker that is easy to use. Labeling is the key to creating a fool-proof system. It increases your effectiveness at work, as well as the independence of others who function within your workspace. Label the placement of items (shelves, files, containers, bins, baskets or drawers), and take the time to label the front and backs of boxes or bins stored on shelves, so that no thought needs to go into storing them again. Hand-held electronic labelers are easy to use and create a neat label for anything.

5. Create a "Take to meeting" bin or folder. Every time you come across or think of something you need to take to your next meeting(s), place it in the bin or folder. According to the Brother P-touch Means Business survey, approximately four in 10 office workers have gone into a work meeting feeling unprepared.

6. Create a folder titled "Pending" for papers waiting for another person's response or action. This folder will help clear off your desk and cork board. Revisit this folder often to make sure the action required or response needed occurred. Set up this folder in your email's inbox for "pending" items there too!

7. Log missed calls. Use a telephone message log or journal to write down voicemail messages left for you and to write down notes during telephone conversations. You'll have a record of all calls and conversations in one organized location.

8. One hour before "closing" time, get your desk in order. This way if you discover an oversight of a task or call, you will still have plenty of time to accomplish it.

So this new year, go ahead, purge the unnecessary, designate places for essentials, go vertical and label, label, label! The organization of your home office will reduce your stress, increase your productivity and free up more time for you.

WAYS TO KEEP COSTS DOWN WHEN YOU WORK FROM HOME

Some easy ways to save when you work out of your house.
by Sara Sutton, CEO & Founder of FlexJobs

After much negotiating (and let's face it, a little pleading on your part) you and your boss designed a work from home arrangement that was ideal for you. Things were working out great—your boss was pleased with your performance and you were more productive than ever—until you realized you were shelling out a lot of money as a remote worker. But working from home can save you money in the long run. Here's how to work it right.

Turn off your equipment. When you worked in the office, you often left your computer on all day—and all night. But you should be more conservative when it comes to your own office equipment. Shutting down your computer, scanner and monitor at the end of the workday will save you extra on your electric bill. It can also extend the life of your equipment, too.

Eat leftovers. Sure, when you were an office gal, you would eat out for lunch with your colleagues every day. After all, who could be bothered schlepping salads and soups into work? Now that you're home, though, raid the fridge—and forego takeout—on your lunch break. And think twice before popping that slice of pizza into the oven, which can use more electricity or gas than a microwave or even a toaster oven. You'll see immediate cost-savings on your bill, and using up leftovers (instead of eating out) will help you keep more of your paycheck in your pocket.

Use fans or portable heaters. When there's a nip in the air, you're cranking up the heat. But it makes no sense to heat the *entire* house when it's just you working from your home office. (The same holds true for central air conditioning, too.) Opt to use a portable fan when it's stuffy inside your office, or a small heater to keep you cozy as you work on those expense reports. Dressing appropriately can also help you feel comfortable, so pile on the layers to help you stay cool—and work hard.

Beyond increased productivity and the ability to work in your yoga pants if you want to, telecommuting can help you save a lot of money, too. Simply adapting to a new work from home style will allow you to see the savings add up fast.

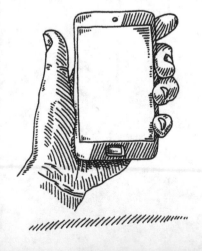

MOM'S 'RAW' POST NAILS 'VALLEYS' OF WORKING MOTHERHOOD IN COVID-19 ERA

The post even caught Jennifer Garner's attention.
by Meredith Bodgas

Offer food and water. Check that no one needs a new diaper/change of clothes/blanket. Put on a movie sure to capture their attention. We all do this dance before joining business calls. Yet no matter how many precautions we take to prevent disruptions while working from home with kids, when we finally focus on our job, it triggers chaos. Kenzi Reddick, a marketer for Wrangler Jeans, has experienced that "flip of the switch moment" with her two young children. And she's pinpointed what triggers it, despite our best preparations.

"The moment I get on a conference call, it's like the diversion of my attention away from them sets them off." Bingo.

"They don't understand being asked to be quiet for 30 minutes so mommy can talk or listen. Or to stay out of the trash can. Or to not ask me for a snack for the 50th time. Or to sit still or share," she continued in her viral Instagram post from May 1.

But the aftermath of everything falling apart with colleagues as an audience takes its toll. After she hung up on one such call, she screamed at her kids "in frustration" (been there) and then sat on the floor and sobbed (been there too).

"And my kids got to bear witness to it," she admitted beside a photo of her mascara-streaked face. (Kudos to Kenzi for putting on makeup these days.) "I documented this because I want to remember the valley as much as I remember the mountain . . . Some days I feel confident and accomplished and other days I just hope I loved well & hard enough. The good thing is, these babies are resilient and forgiving. And despite the moments where I am lacking attention or patience, I am still their favorite person. They knew my frustration was directed to them and they both cried and came directly to hug me . . . Not my proudest moment as a mama but it was a raw one."

This is practically a daily scene in my house. It's not my kids' fault that work is entirely incompatible with the kind of care they need at 6- and 2-years-old. It's not my kids' fault that they're programmed to seek my attention as soon as I can't give it. And it's definitely not my kids' fault that a pandemic has pissed all over their previously happy (though hectic) routines—and the comfort of that familiarity is gone.

But as actress Jennifer Garner pointed out in a comment to Kenzi's post, "It is so helpful to see the truth, even for kids. You caught them up on the other side with so much love—they just got a lesson in emotion being ok and in the passing of frustration and sadness. Tomorrow will for sure be better ♡ ♡ ♡ ♡."

Let's hope so.

Screentime Ideas for Kids at Home

Sometimes you just need to hand your kid a tablet while you get work done—and we don't judge! Here are some age-appropriate free and low-cost suggestions they'll love:

Ages 2 to 5

Even toddlers tire of Blippi. Here are some slightly more under-the-radar options to break out when you're trying to work from home with kids.

Mighty Machines, YouTube: If you're not already familiar with this 1990s Canadian show, then clearly you haven't gone very deep into a "kids trucks" playlist on YouTube. But you'll be glad you've found it now. There are 36 episodes, about a half-hour long each, in which all kinds of real trucks, from fire engines to tow trucks to sanitation trucks, get voiced by offscreen actors and take kids through a regular day for them. Good luck getting the catchy, gritty theme song out of your head.

SciShow Kids, YouTube: Even though these videos are short—about three to five minutes each—there are four years' worth of mini science lessons, many on tough-to-answer questions little kids have, such as why do we get dizzy and where did the moon come from. They're part animated and all hosted by engaging, enthusiastic mom Jessi Knudsen Castañeda. If you overhear it, you'll probably find yourself learning some new things too.

Khan Academy Kids, available for iPhone, iPad, Google Play, and Amazon Fire: If the name Khan Academy rings a bell, it's because they've had K-12 educational materials for years. But they recently launched a learning program for the pre-K and kindergarten set. Just like its forerunner, the interactive and truly enjoyable learning materials are all free.

Ages 5 to 8

Elementary-school-age kids might have online lessons with their teachers, but there's still that after-school time to fill. Try these videos and apps.

GoNoodle Family: Your kids might already know the movement and mindfulness app from school (many educators use it across the country). Even if you don't have a login through their class, you can use it at home. It's like an especially little kid-appropriate *Dance, Dance Revolution* with easy-to-follow themed moves set to songs children love—or will grow to love. But there are also breathing and yoga exercises that encourage calm, something you'll all need after many days inside.

Mr. DeMaio, YouTube: New Jersey teacher Michael DeMaio has a knack for explaining complicated concepts in a laugh-out-loud funny manner. He mixes live-action with animation, a la Roger Rabbit—and seamlessly works in '80s and '90s references millennial parents enjoy. There's math, history, and lots of science in his 70 videos, which range from a couple minutes long to about as long as a standard TV episode.

Get more media suggestions:
CommonSense.org, the nonprofit dedicated to telling parents and educators what they need to know about media kids might consume, has lists of the best movies, TV shows, books, apps, websites, music, and more for children. You can filter by age group and media type and, for movies and shows, browse by streaming service.

ANOTHER MOM CALLED ME 'LAZY' FOR QUITTING HOMESCHOOLING. HERE'S WHAT SHE SHOULD KNOW

A pandemic is a pretty awful time to judge anyone's parenting.
by Meredith Bodgas

Working Mother shared a story about homeschooling tips in May 2020 that readers found very helpful the first time we shared it on Facebook in March. Two months into the U.S. lockdown, though, the ideas were no longer resonating.

"Great, so the advice is, work full time during the week, add in three meals a day, snacks, breaking up fights, making suggestions for entertainment etc, then spend your weekend homeschooling so you don't feel guilty that you couldn't fit it in during the week! Then wonder why you feel like you aren't coping and nobody is happy," wrote one commenter.

"It's the 'oh you need tips on homeschooling' attitude that I find very unhelpful. I know many homeschool moms. None of them have a full time business hours-driven job. Because homeschooling IS a job in itself! It isn't that we need to figure out homeschooling! It's that it's 'unattainable parenting standards,'" wrote another.

"Though I'm sure well intended . . . I have the utmost respect for homeschooling moms (like, for real), but can't relate to the overwhelm of expert advice being thrown and better resonate with those who are unexpectedly working FT with kids & schooling at home at the same time," wrote yet another.

Thing is, I, the editor-in-chief, agreed with them. I was no longer implementing the suggestions from the article, as instructive as I found them the first time. So I told them so.

"We hear you all loud and clear and appreciate the feedback," I started. "I've personally given up on forcing homeschooling . . . We all have to do whatever is going to help us survive."

You'd think I'd just admitted that I stopped feeding my kids because of the comment my reply solicited.

"I don't doubt you have given up on helping with learning. I mean how else could you prioritize writing pithy articles and self-serving social media posts if you didn't. It's lazy parenting to 'give up.'"

Another working mom wrote that.

Now, every brand whose social media I've ever managed has had trolls. But that comment wasn't just trolling—it was the kind of sanctimonious (or "sanctimommious," as another commenter pointed out) judgment that perpetuates the nastiest mommy wars that achieve nothing productive.

This particular troll comments a lot, not just on our Facebook page but on others. Frankly, I'm impressed that a mom with a job who hasn't given up on homeschooling has time for that.

As impressive as that might be, there's one thing I'm sure of: Whatever kind of parenting any working mom is doing right now that doesn't leave her children sick, destitute or traumatized is good parenting.

Call me—and others who have stopped homeschooling or even distance learning—whatever you want. We're expected to do our jobs perfectly without childcare for weeks on end, while going without our usual stress relievers, such as seeing friends and family and having date nights out at restaurants. And many of us have had to do this while sick or while caring for sick kids. Prioritizing our mental health over, say, forcing unwilling, anxious kids to do 12 assignments a day is how we're going to get through a pandemic without lasting, irreparable damage to ourselves or our families. Maybe it's lazy. But it's also smart.

I'm going to be very vulnerable with you all right now: I'm struggling. My working husband and I have tried all the tricks out there and we're still struggling. Those who aren't struggling? Wow. You're amazing. Those who are? Yeah, this is hard. No one was prepared for this. There's no playbook for this. So, we have one request of those who aren't struggling: Don't try to make us feel worse for having a tough time and making hard decisions that help us stay alive.

In our little family of four, we have mental health issues and behavioral disorders. We are getting virtual help. But—surprise!—there isn't a therapy or medication that makes a pandemic disappear, to paraphrase my therapist friend. We all fare better with loving reassurance about our lowered expectations, not wicked shaming.

Isn't that true of parenting in general, pandemic or not? Judging doesn't make anyone—judge or judged—a better mother. And it's depressing that these public parenting pissing contests are usually between moms, not dads. Still, no one should reverse course on what works for their family because of what someone on the internet says. *Working Mother* advice included.

How to Set Your Kid Up for Virtual Learning Success

If your child's school is virtual or you've decided to homeschool, here are some ideas for helping them learn from home:

1. Have morning stand-up to discuss that day's rough schedule. Kids do better when they're mentally prepared for the day ahead, particularly if their routine changes day by day.

2. Ask your children's teachers to set priorities for their daily schoolwork, and provide honest feedback about what's doable and not. Have these conversations regularly. Ask for a list of apps, passwords, and instructions for their learning platforms, and share it with your partner or caregivers.

3. Set up worksheets and apps that require guidance only when you're free to give it.

4. Make their learning zone feel special. Choose a designated space for their desk that's ideally in an area with fewer distractions (i.e., not the kitchen table). Surround it with educational posters. Have their frequently used supplies, like pencils and erasers, handy. Hang up a calendar as well as their daily schedule, so they can easily see the plan for the day and week.

VP MOM'S 'I'M NOT SORRY' CREDO IS JUST WHAT WORKING PARENTS NEED RIGHT NOW

Read this. Print this. Show it to every working mom you know.
by Quinn Fish

Working moms often struggle with the feeling that we're not giving enough to our kids *or* our career. With the added stressors of the novel coronavirus pandemic, that guilt is heavier than ever.

We are working from home *and* homeschooling our kids at the same time—while feeling exhausted and unable to enjoy this extra family time. No wonder the pressures of the pandemic are especially burdensome for working moms. Luckily, one mom gave us the reminder we all need that our priorities are in the right place.

Kimberly Burck, vice president of sales at Mason Dixie Biscuit Co. and mom of two boys, took to LinkedIn with a story of how she's embracing the fact that motherhood takes precedence. Instead of feeling guilty or embarrassed that her kids have "accidentally joined 70% of [her] video calls," she decided to be whole-heartedly unapologetic.

"Somewhere along this quarantine I stopped apologizing. I'm not sorry for the interruption because I'm not sorry for being a Mom. It is why I work so hard and care so much. I love what I do and I love being a Mom. I'm not sorry," Kimberly wrote.

Often, working moms are made to feel like they have to set strict boundaries between their parenting and employee duties, but the pandemic has shown that it simply isn't possible.

Whether our little ones need a snack or a hug, good employers understand that we can't be in full work mode 24/7 these days. True leadership means acknowledging employees' realities and being empathetic that we're not working the same way we were pre-pandemic.

As Kimberly said, working moms love what we do and we love being moms. We shouldn't have to apologize for either.

CEO MOM NAILS WHY WORKING FROM HOME DOESN'T MEAN EMPLOYEES ARE AVAILABLE 24/7

True leaders know that most people want to do their best,
and they need support and empathy at this time.
by Quinn Fish

With offices and schools closed indefinitely throughout most of the US, working from home while homeschooling is the new norm for many parents. It's safe to say we're not working in the same way we were pre-pandemic.

Some managers seem to think that our new virtual work world means we should be able to answer calls and emails immediately, at any hour. It's true we don't have in-person meetings, daycare pick-up or evening obligations right now, but parents aren't any more available than we otherwise would be. In fact, with our homeschooling and childcare duties, we're less available than we've ever been.

Robynn Storey, CEO of Storeyline Resumes and mom of one, took to LinkedIn with a story of a boss's unrealistic expectations and how that can affect a team.

"I just had a conversation with a new client . . . a frustrated professional who has a boss that thinks because his team is 'working from home' they should be available to answer his calls/emails day and night, and respond accordingly," Robynn wrote. "My client is getting blasted with requests and his boss is getting pissed when he is not answering within five minutes."

Robynn's client isn't just working from home but he's also home-schooling his kids, taking care of his parents and trying to split it all with his spouse. "His sole focus 24/7 is not on his job, nor should it be."

She wrote that her client's boss is piling on the complaints about the team's lack of availability and preparedness, going so far as to threaten cuts. But the stressors of the pandemic should show managers there are more important things than their team members' yields, Robynn added.

"True leaders know that most people want to do their best, and they need support and empathy at this time. No one does a good job when they are being screamed at...," she wrote. "Everyone needs to chill out a bit."

As stressful as these times are for companies struggling to stay afloat amidst a looming recession and skyrocketing unemployment rates, Robynn's story reminds us that humanity must always come first. Showing your team you can acknowledge and accommodate their tricky new reality does wonders for team spirit. Show this to your manager who wants to know why you can't work till 9 p.m. while you're stretched thinner than you ever thought possible.

CHILDLESS CEO TO PARENTS WITH KIDS ON VIDEO CALLS: 'THANK YOU, IT'S LIKE A BREATH OF FRESH AIR'

More company leaders should think this way.
by Quinn Fish

With kids and parents stuck at home due to the novel coronavirus pandemic, video call interruptions are the new norm for working moms. Luckily, some managers get it.

Now that parents have been homeschooling while working from home for a few months, we've grown accustomed to distractions. Still, the interruptions can lead to feelings of guilt and unnecessary stress for parents while on the clock.

Robert Sadow, the CEO and co-founder of Scoop, a rideshare enterprise company in the San Francisco Bay area, took to LinkedIn with his thoughts on the little faces and voices he sees on video call meetings.

"A lot of us are on video conferences most of the day. It is taxing, exhausting and frankly a bit monotonous.

"When you start a meeting and someone has their child with them, it's like a breath of fresh air. We can't help but smile as they interact with their parents, ask questions, or point at the screen.

"It's also a really important reminder of the big picture and the many facets of the lives of our team members," Robert wrote.

Though Robert doesn't have any kids, his refreshing take on accepting the reality of working parenthood in the COVID-19 era should set an example for managers everywhere. Further, he emphasized that the workplace needs to acknowledge what team members might be dealing with at home.

"To all the #parents: I don't have children, so I can't pretend to understand just how hard it is to balance #work and everything happening at home," Robert wrote. "But I can say #thankyou for the little bits of joy you bring to some of my meetings."

Let this be a reminder that the next time your little ones pop into your video meeting, instead of scrambling to shoo them away, consider the fact that they just might be brightening someone's day. Stay strong, mama.

IT PAINS ME, BUT MY HUSBAND'S STABLE JOB IS MORE IMPORTANT THAN MINE DURING THIS PANDEMIC

We need his higher salary and better benefits more than ever.
by Juliet Diamond-Ciro

"Because Dad's job is more imp—" I stopped myself. I couldn't believe what I'd almost told my son, who was wondering why he had to stay with me while I joined a video meeting. I didn't recognize the woman who proudly wears her working mom badge, who's passionate about equalizing gendered imbalances in all relationships, who advocates for women to succeed professionally. Surely, she would never think that her husband's job was more valuable than her own, let alone tell that to her impressionable 5-year-old.

I didn't have to finish the word. My perceptive son no doubt already sensed that his father's job took precedence over mine in the COVID era. He and his little brother spend much more time with me during business hours over their dad.

Try as we might every night through calendar acrobatics, my husband and I frequently wind up with meetings that overlap. And just about every time that's happened, I've taken my video call from our living room with the kids around, while my husband has the relative child-free peace our basement affords. That's because even though his company is, theoretically, as family friendly as mine, the truth is his job is more crucial for our finances than mine in every way. So that's the one we put both our efforts toward keeping.

Not so long ago, our base salaries were pretty evenly matched. Then COVID hit, and I took a nearly 15 percent salary reduction. Our companies both matched our 401k contributions. Now, only his does. His employer promised not to lay off a single soul for 90 days. Mine shed several long-term employees and ominously admitted that more cuts were to come. He might not get his entire annual bonus, but his company guaranteed a good chunk of it whether or not his team hits their goals during the pandemic. I got a small bonus once in three years. His employer's health insurance was always far superior to mine, and nothing has changed there.

Sure, I could say it's because women, in general, are more poorly compensated than men. But it's also because he has an engineering job at a successful tech company, which attracts more men—perhaps because historically, that field hasn't been kind to women—and I'm in the flailing media industry, with plenty of women around, though not many at the top making the decisions that make or break the business.

When he gets an invite to secure a deal worth 10 to 100 times more than the kinds I play a role in, yeah, I'm going to be joining my call with the little ones jumping on the couch next to me. When his childless manager wants to talk one-on-one with him at the same time my kid-loving manager wants to check in with me, guess where the boys are: with me. And when we both need focused time to tackle a challenging work issue, he gets first dibs for scheduling it.

We're putting our family first, but it feels like we're putting his career first, and mine a distant second. I don't resent my husband—I'm grateful he works for such a wonderful employer that keeps our family afloat, allowing me to do what I love even though it's not as stable or lucrative. But I wish I could do what I love during this crisis without having to simultaneously fulfill the bulk of the responsibilities of a stay-at-home parent. And just as much, I wish my sons could see that Mom's job is just as important as Dad's.

I know I'm not the only woman making this calculation right now. Women have been putting husbands, kids and practically everyone else but themselves first since time immemorial. Despite doing what's best for my family, I'm guilty of perpetuating a cycle that holds moms back. (No wonder working moms' anxiety is sky-high right now.) But if I've learned anything during these trying times, it's this: We have to go easy on ourselves. We're doing our best. In my case, that means I'm doing what I can to show my boys that women's work—both the paid and unpaid time—matters. Even if I'm too busy to traditionally homeschool them, they're absorbing this key lesson. That just might help them end the cycle one day.

DAD'S KEYBOARD HACK HELPS HIM STAY PRODUCTIVE WITH HIS TODDLER ON HIS LAP

There's just one caveat.
by Maricar Santos

A Wisconsin dad has a simple solution for doing your job with a little one nearby.

Andrew Metz has two boys—an 8-year-old and a 6-year-old—and a toddler daughter. Due to the coronavirus pandemic, he has been working from home as regional vice president of Zywave, an insurance agency software company.

In a LinkedIn post from last week, the father shared how he manages to be productive with his youngest in the room. He sets up a keyboard that's unplugged and has her "work" alongside him.

The arrangement allows him to concentrate while keeping his child occupied.

The hack quickly gained a lot of attention on LinkedIn, racking up over 20,000 reactions.

According to some commenters, Andrew's idea isn't new, but it *is* effective.

"I did this with my daughter a month ago. She [has] seen me working the keys so I took an old keyboard and she just started pecking away," one user wrote.

But beware: Kiddos catch on very quickly.

One comment read, "It doesn't work as long as you hope it will. I've gone as far as plugging them into another machine so it lights up since the little bugger is so dang sharp and realizes it wasn't plugged in."

In an update to his post today, Andrew shared that his daughter has moved out of his office and now has her own "workstation." It sounds like he will need to tweak his hack very soon!

Hey, we'll take whatever help we can get, even if it's just for the time being.

3 Ways to Minimize Interruptions While You're Working

You love your children, but you don't love the 97 times they demand your attention during your workday. Here's how to keep the distractions to a minimum:

1. Find Free Virtual Learning Opportunities
Thankfully, there's a plethora of free websites and programs available to keep kids learning. Check out the website for your favorite museum or park—many are now offering free virtual tours. Big names like Scholastic, PBS Kids, *Highlights*, and *National Geographic* all offer up free activities and videos. Mom groups on Facebook and other social media sites can be great resources for finding virtual opportunities hosted by your local libraries and other community centers.

2. Give Them Visual Cues about Your Availability
Got a work call? Saying, "I'll be off in half an hour," doesn't mean much to a 4-year-old. If you have one of those color-coded clocks, intended for letting little ones know not to get out of bed

before a human hour, repurpose it to let them know when you'll be able to give them your undivided attention. No special clock? Timers and digital clocks (with instructions such as "when this number 2 becomes a 3") can help.

3. Make Snacks and Toys Accessible

One way to do this: Consider prepping snacks and lunch for little hands ahead of the workday and keeping those meals accessible so kids can help themselves while you work from home. Give your children (age 3+) clear instructions, say, whenever they're hungry, they can take one item from the lowest fridge shelf. They must shut the fridge door behind them and eat their snack at the table.

The same accessibility rule goes for activities. If they can play on a tablet, make sure it's charged and within reach, and they are well-versed in operating it themselves. Put out toys, crafts, and other playtime supplies that don't require adult assembly at their eye level.

THE 10 BEST RESOURCES FOR FINDING A WORK-FROM-HOME JOB

Make sure to check these websites before your next job search.
by Joseph Barberio

Working from home can be a dream setup for working moms thanks to the flexibility it provides. But it's not always easy to find employers who are willing to let you telecommute, or remote jobs that match your skill set.

If you've had trouble finding a work-from-home job, then look no further. We've rounded up the best resources available across the Internet for helping working moms find the perfect job. They include helpful websites, specific job boards and even networks that match you up with a potential employer.

1. Liveops

Giant call center buildings are becoming a thing of the past. Companies now use remote workers to operate the phones and assist customers. That's where Liveops comes in. The Scottsdale, AZ-based tech company hires remote workers as customer service "contractors" who then get matched with companies, according to their schedule and skills. Most companies pay a per-talk-minute rate, so the more calls you take, the more you earn.

2. Karat

Who better to evaluate the best talent in technology and engineering than people who are already established in the fields? If you're an expert in these arenas, consider Karat: The company helps tech and engineering companies hire rockstar employees by utilizing experts to interview them. (That would be you.) The interviews can be done remotely and are on your schedule. It can even be done as a lucrative full-time job or as a side hustle.

3. FlexJobs

FlexJobs is the one-stop-shop for finding jobs that allow flexible work, including working from home. It screens jobs before posting them to guarantee that they are actual opportunities and not work-from-home scams. You can also research companies on the website and see what kind of remote jobs they have offered in the past.

4. HireMyMom.com

HireMyMom understands how important remote work can be for mothers. The job board lists opportunities specifically for working moms and the skills they can provide. Businesses post jobs ranging from full-time work to freelance projects.

5. Prokanga

Prokanga is a job network that connects qualified members with flexible work in specialized fields. Large companies in need of finance and marketing consultants go directly to them to find and hire the best candidates. While network members often get matched up with consulting or temporary gigs, it is possible to get a full-time job.

6. The Second Shift

"The (work)force is female," states The Second Shift on its company mission page. The website put employers in touch with women in a variety of fields who are looking for remote work projects to tackle.

Members "pitch" themselves and their skills to companies and, once they've got a match, The Second Shift will help handle all of the employment paperwork.

7. The Mom Project

This digital talent marketplace connects women with world-class companies and is particularly dedicated to helping moms who've taken a career break to care for their kids. On their site, you can search for remote and/or part-time jobs.

8. Guru

Have a specific marketable skill? Guru lets you post your resume or portfolio along with other employment information (like your schedule and rates), so companies on the lookout for freelancers can find you. There is also a section of the site where you can search through listings that match up with your skills.

9. Rat Race Rebellion

While Rat Race Rebellion is home to plenty of tips and advice for landing a work-from-home gig, the website may be best known for its "Big List" of remote jobs. The site is constantly adding new opportunities when they are made available. Their daily newsletter also keeps subscribers informed of new jobs, so you never miss a single update.

10. Skip the Drive

Skip the Drive hosts a large job board with posts in a wide range of fields, but it's best feature might be its "Telecommuting Calculator." The tool allows users to figure out how much they save by working at home in lieu of commuting. It's just a little bit more motivation to look for a remote job!

Members shift the tasks to and return it to companies each once they've got a minute. The second shift will help be life all of the employees' paperwork.

7. The Night Shift

Be flexible to your schedule arrangements. Adjust with each parent company and reduce everyday schedule to help pay with time to arrange a schedule for each for their kids. Consider that you can share or arrange other starting plans.

8. Crib

Don't specialize people skills. Good tips for you put your team feeling or part time work and other employment help them to keep the schedule. A cost to obtain in the workplace even though it can find you. If there is a section, they are where you come to work through using which will no wrap your skills.

9. Keep Your Job Hunt

Will for Real Websites are hoping plenty of tips and even those landing a website in long gap, the website to the best, I wrote through digital from others jobs. The ones constantly posting new opportunities when more is available. That they revisit the also keep some resources from landing a new job so you never miss a single update.

10. It's right

Consider Day to be future that your resources it will save you money, but it's not just about working from home. The real bonus comes to work out how much they save by staying at home behind to of considering. It's worth it. Some money save for to like it as a work shift.

3 OUT-OF-THE-BOX TIPS FOR BEATING THE WORK-FROM-HOME BLUES

Sure, most working moms wish they could work at home most of the time. But there are pitfalls. What to do?
by Marisa LaScala

Working from home has its perks, but you can miss the camaraderie of an office—and your co-workers might miss you too. A recent study reveals that working from home can increase a sense of loneliness in remote workers and their in-office counterparts equally. But you needn't feel so cut off. Beyond Skype and Google Hangouts, try these strategies.

Get face time (even if you don't want to). University of Chicago psychologists found that loneliness triggers electrical activity in the brain that might lead to an urge to isolate even further. Break the cycle with increased social interactions—and accept that invite for coffee.

Take time to meditate. Those who practice mindful meditation feel less lonely than those who don't, according to a Carnegie Mellon University study.

Get a museum membership. Yes, really! Researchers at University College London Hospital found that museum visits lead to reduced social isolation as well as decreased anxiety and increased self-esteem—which will make you a better worker overall.

WHAT HAPPENS IF
YOUR BOSS WON'T LET YOU
WORK FROM HOME IN A CRISIS?

Here's what to do if you don't feel safe going to work.
by Debi Yadegari, JD, Founder and CEO, Villyge

More and more businesses are advising or requiring employees to work from home. While this offers a modicum of relief for some, there remains a large contingent of the workforce that either (1) does not have a job that lends itself to the ability to work remotely, or (2) works for a company that, even in the face of the coronavirus, will not permit its employees to work from home. If you find yourself experiencing the same, what are your options? And how might you prevail?

Absent an internal policy or statutory right permitting someone to work from home (e.g., under a leave law or reasonable accommodation law), there is not much an employee can do when an employer says "no." They can submit, try their powers of persuasion or simply walk out. That said, we have suggestions for navigating path No. 2 and a few considerations for option No. 3.

First, if you have a role within your company that you could handle from home, begin with a dialogue with your employer. Like any negotiation, preparation is key. For the best chance of success and prevailing upon your boss, be sure to have all of your information in good order. Winging it will probably not get you very far. Find examples of companies in your city and your industry allowing employees to work remotely. You will likely find many.

Next, have a detailed plan of how you would achieve your work objectives from home. Technology has advanced tremendously in the past few years and the capabilities are unprecedented. Also address how you would collaborate with team members and external parties, as appropriate. The employer needs to know that workflow and the bottom line will not suffer.

The idea of an indefinite work-from-home period may be daunting for some employers. Offer to try it for a limited period, such as two to three days, or even just a day. And then agree to reassess the situation, together with your employer. From there, you can extend the period a few days at a time and continue to monitor the situation, encouraging employer feedback.

Follow up your conversation with a written memo reiterating your plan and addressing the reasons you have requested to work from home: the CDC is recommending "social distancing"; your commute requires the use of mass transit; you do not want to increase your exposure to possible contagions; and you have a duty to advocate for the safety of your family. Draw the picture that it would be better for you, and your company, to have you working from home right now by focusing on the productivity piece of the puzzle.

Assuming it is still a no-go for your boss, you would have written proof that you tried to initiate a collaborative dialogue with your boss and were willing to maintain your workload and responsibilities, in the face of crisis. But being concerned for the safety and well-being of your family during this precarious time, you had no option but to leave the office. That pattern of facts might come in handy down the line, should you face termination or disciplinary actions.

Under the occupational safety and health laws (commonly known as OSHA laws), employers are prohibited from terminating an employee who in good faith refuses to expose themselves to a dangerous job condition and who has no reasonable alternative but to avoid the workplace. However, the condition causing your fear must be objectively reasonable—it can't simply be the *potential* for unsafe working conditions. Section 7 of the National Labor Relations Act also provides protections against discharge if an employee's refusal is part of a concerted protest against unsafe working conditions.

Those same legal protections might be afforded to you if you're unable to work from home due to your type of job and/or role within the company. While you might not be entitled to wages for missed work, there might (at least) be an argument for job preservation. That is, once it's safe for you to return to work, you'll still have your old role to which to return.

These are uncertain times for everyone. Employees and employers, alike, are encouraged to engage in proactive conciliatory discussions and recognize that what we do, and how we respond, now will have long-term implications for both companies and workers.

SHOW THIS TO YOUR MANAGER: PEOPLE WHO WORK FROM HOME HAVE BEEN PROVEN TO BE MORE PRODUCTIVE

Another reason why remote jobs are a win-win.
by Joseph Barberio

For many working moms, snagging a remote job is a dream scenario that allows them to achieve more of a work-life balance. Unfortunately, the biggest obstacle in their way is often managers who are skeptical about the productivity of telecommuters.

However, a new study published in the journal *New Technology, Work and Employment* has found that people who work from home actually tend to be more productive—even when they are parents with kids.

The study surveyed about 15,000 people in Great Britain in 2001, 2006 and 2012 on their working habits and found that remote workers are more likely to put in extra effort. Alan Felstead, professor at Cardiff University's School of Social Science and co-author of the study, says that it may have to do with them trying to show that they are not lazy.

"The evidence suggests that remote workers are over-compensating to prove to their colleagues they are not in their pajamas at home and prove to their employers that they are a safe pair of hands willing to go the extra mile for the discretion an employer gives them to work at home or in a remote location," said Felstead in an interview with the *Daily Mail*.

About a quarter of participants in fixed workplaces reported that they were willing to put in extra work or hours for their jobs, while 39 percent of remote workers said that they would. And 73 percent of the remote workers said they put more effort into their work in general, as opposed to 69 percent of in-office workers.

The study does note that some of the remote workers did report having trouble with stopping work because they don't have a commute to signify the end of the day.

"Our study also shows that employers benefit from increased effort as workers strive to show that working remotely is not a slacker's charter," said Felstead. "However, remote workers find greater difficulty in redrawing the boundaries between work and non-work life."

The results of the study also hold true for parents with children at home while working, according to Felstead. So you can proudly show these findings to your boss and explain that working from home will be beneficial to both you and your company.

MOMS WHO WORK FROM HOME ARE MORE SUCCESSFUL THAN MOMS WHO DON'T

A new study concludes that remote companies help women avoid office politics and advance.

by Joseph Barberio

From flexible hours to cutting out a commute, work-from-home jobs have obvious benefits for working moms, but it turns out they may come with an unexpected perk: an easier climb up the career ladder.

A new study, conducted by Remote.co, found that businesses with sizable remote workforces tend to have higher numbers of female executives. Of the 128 mostly or completely remote companies surveyed, 19 percent had female CEOs and 28 percent had women CEOs, founders or presidents. And 72 percent of the female leaders and executives surveyed were working parents.

The numbers get even more impressive when they examined companies where every employee is a telecommuter. In these 77 companies, 29 percent had either a female CEO, founder or president.

This stands in stark contrast to the rest of the country. For example, only 5.2 percent of companies in the S&P 500 and 6.4 percent of those in the *Fortune* 500 list had female CEOs last year.

The study's authors speculate that the reason the numbers are so high is because women at remote or mostly remote companies are more likely to be fairly evaluated.

"It's because remote work requires companies to focus on the most important aspects of work—productivity, progress, results—rather than less important things like face time in the office, office politics, traditional notions of what leadership 'looks like,' popularity or likability, or hours spent at your desk," they write.

Alice Hendricks, CEO of software company Jackson River, agrees that working from home allows women to "not have to spend so much of their lives playing the part of a leader who looks a certain way, and instead just get on with the business of running teams, producing results and being the leaders that their companies need."

The flexibility at these jobs may also factor into the success of these women, and especially moms. "It is extremely challenging for women at the top of brick-and-mortar companies to meet the strict demands of a work schedule that allows for little flexibility," said Ellen Grealish, co-founder and partner of staffing agency FlexProfessionals.

The study also notes that the percentage of startups in the United States with female founders hasn't increased since 2012. One remote executive theorizes that women may soon capitalize on the advantages of working from home and create their own opportunities.

"I think that's why many women are saying 'enough is enough' and starting their own ventures virtually, where they have the control over their work schedule, hours and location," said Sanda Lewis, founder and director of virtual assistant staffing firm Worldwide 101. "I very much believe it's the future of work, and all these women are truly the pioneers."

THE TRUTH BEHIND WHAT I'M DOING WHEN I WORK FROM HOME

Yes, I'm wearing pajama pants. Yes, I'm more productive.
by Meredith Bodgas

In the past three weeks, I've been to the office one time. I don't state that fact to brag. I actually would like to talk to my coworkers in person instead of staring at my son's toys and husband's clothes strewn about our living room. But a combination of holidays, my preschooler coming down with a virus, snowpocalypses, pregnancy-induced nausea, pregnancy-induced insomnia and pregnancy-induced symphysis pubis dysfunction (which makes taking a step feel like someone is stabbing me in the bikini line) has kept me mostly house-bound. I am extraordinarily lucky to have a job that can be done well from a remote location. I recognize that I'm even more fortunate to have a manager who allows me to work from my house. Despite medical warnings, I am so grateful to hold a sedentary position.

That being said, I know colleagues wonder, "Where's Meredith?" I would guess some, at least at previous jobs, think, "How nice for her not to have to come in while the rest of us are actually doing work." But the truth is I work harder and for longer durations on my work-from-home days.

I wake up around 7:30 a.m. which, admittedly, is a nice reprieve from my 6:00 a.m. alarm time on in-office days. I either take a gloriously long 15-minute shower in my quiet house or, if it hasn't been that long, throw on comfy clothes without hosing myself off. If I have video calls, I make sure that my top is work appropriate. I even put on a bra, albeit a wireless one. The pants are always of the yoga/pajama variety.

I head to my kitchen table for breakfast and start working, even though it's not quite 8:00 a.m. I respond to emails that came in after my embarrassingly early bedtime, look for news stories to cover on workingmother.com and set the lineup of articles and assignments for the morning.

In the good old pre-pregnancy days, when my pelvis was still aligned with my legs, I'd walk to my home office, about 15 feet from my dining room table. These days, though, getting to the couch just five feet away is a struggle. That's where I park my butt and my laptop, along with water and a snack to limit the amount of times I get up.

I check how the previous day's stories performed, schedule a morning Facebook post or two and start approving my team's story ideas as they come in, starting at about 9. I set the rest of the day's article lineup by about 10 a.m.

Today, I'm done editing a piece by 10:15, and move on to editing another, or writing one.

At this point, I might have to use the restroom. I bring this up because the 10 feet to walk there and back takes me about five minutes, round-trip. Anyone who doubts my productivity is right to in this one regard. Then again, the trip to and from my workplace restroom takes easily double this amount of time.

I usually have a call to jump on next. And when I'm off, I finish writing or editing another story (today, this is it).

I pause to prep my lunch, reheating leftovers or making a sandwich because standing to do real cooking is about as appealing as running a marathon in my condition. When my food's ready, I usually have another story to edit—which I do while eating because I don't want to hold up my team. One time during lunch, I watched an episode of Netflix's *Atypical* (so good, you should see it) because I didn't have anything pressing to address. I almost got to the end when an IM with a link to look over came in.

There are usually two more calls to take. And in between, I edit a magazine story or two. I might approve a magazine layout or some photos as well.

I don't pick up my son's toys. I sure as hell don't address my husband's clothes. The laundry remains undone, my dishes unclean. I do, however, refill my Brita because I drink water like it's my job these days, and I am working, after all. I exchange two emails with my mother and two IMs with my husband. There are many more IMs between me and my colleagues. I retrieve my mail only if I'm expecting a package and it's exciting enough to warrant the grueling seven-foot trip to the front door. I check in on the app that allows me to see what my son is doing at preschool but once. And I return a call about changing my next doctor's appointment. I resist the urge to free my struggling Roomba from some spiderweb-like wires. It shouts, "Error, error," and I keep working. My personal time, including the treacherous bathroom jaunts, amounts to about 30 to 45 minutes. Still, 5:00 rolls around swiftly.

Since I'm home, I don't need to log off yet to make daycare pickup in time. So I'll edit another online story and check our Facebook posts for the upcoming evening and early morning, duties I would do during my train ride home. I answer more emails. I keep doing everything I can until 6:30 p.m. when, if my husband doesn't have to work late, he walks through the door with the little boy who lights up my life and makes me stumble over his playthings.

My work-from-home hours are roughly 8:00 a.m. to 6:30 p.m. I'm not straightening up or getting my nails done. But I'm certainly not complaining. I treasure work-from-home days because of the extra hour-and-a-half of sleep, the stairs I don't have to climb during my commute and the proximity to a private toilet. But for anyone who suspects a mom isn't doing much for her job when she works from home, I hope this sets them straight.

HOW TO PROTECT YOUR KIDS' MENTAL HEALTH WHEN THEY FEEL ISOLATED

Doctors say you can do six things right now to help your children cope.
by Lauren Ramakrishna

It's a tough time for everyone—children included.

As COVID-19 first spread across the US in early 2020, parents' main concern became protecting their kids' health. While masking and social distancing have gone a long way to help ensure the physical health of many children and adults in this country, families report a worrying decline in mental health, particularly now.

ParentsTogether Action, a national parent-led non-profit, recently conducted a survey that revealed just how much families are struggling to handle life in the pandemic. In addition to financial struggles (61 percent of respondents said they have lost income since the beginning of the pandemic), 47 percent of parents revealed that their kids' mental health has gotten worse or much worse since this past summer, while a troubling 62 percent of parent respondents worry about their families' ability to make it through the winter months mentally or emotionally.

Those responses mirror recent statistics released by the Centers for Disease Control that show a spike in mental health-related Emergency Department visits by pediatric patients in 2020.

According to the report, "Compared with 2019, the proportion of mental health-related visits for children aged 5 to 11 and 12 to 17 years increased approximately 24 percent and 31 percent, respectively."

The results of ParentTogether Action's survey don't surprise Abigail Schlesinger, MD, the chief of Child & Adolescent Psychiatry and Integrated Care at UPMC Western Psychiatric Hospital and UPMC Children's Hospital of Pittsburgh, who has witnessed an increase in pandemic-related mental health issues in children and their parents. "It's been a long time that we've been in the pandemic, and now we don't have all of the outlets that we had in the summer," she says.

Nekeshia Hammond, a licensed psychologist and owner of Hammond Psychology & Associates, PA, cites a number of factors that can contribute to mental health challenges for kids this year, including social isolation, changes in school environment, loss of stability in routines, and worries about getting sick with COVID-19.

"Children are certainly soaking up all the stress for their personal lives, the families' stress and the societal distress on a whole," Dr. Hammond says.

How to Spot Mental Health Declines in Kids

You can determine how well your children are coping with the stress in their lives by monitoring their behavior. Some of the telltale signs that indicate your child is struggling with his or her mental health are persistent changes in mood or behavior, changes in appetite, sleep troubles, changes in grades, disconnecting from family and peers, and difficulty concentrating.

While teenagers have the ability to tell you when and why they are struggling, it's important to give them some control over how and where they tell you, advises Dr. Schlesinger. When you notice your teen is struggling, "You need to check in and ask when they want to talk about it," she says.

Behavioral shifts in younger kids are a typical indicator of difficulty managing a stressful environment. If you notice increased anxiety, rage or behavioral problems in your younger child, that's an indication that their mental health is suffering and it requires some level of connection or intervention.

The most alarming behavior for parents to watch out for is discussion of self-harm. Data collected between January and September 2020 by nonprofit Mental Health America revealed that more than half of the 11- to 17-year-olds surveyed reported having thoughts of suicide or self-harm. "If your kid expresses thoughts about wanting to die or hopelessness, you should take that very seriously," says Dr. Schlesinger. "You should get help right away."

How to Help Your Kids Right Now

It's natural for parents to worry about how their kids are handling life during the pandemic. But there are specific strategies you can adopt right now to help you and your kids cope.

1. Spend one-on-one time with your kids.

Kids appreciate "special time" with their parents (yes, even teens who might have you believe otherwise). Try to spend even just 5 to 10 minutes per day connecting with your child. Allow them to choose the activity and make sure your phone is on silent so you can remain totally engaged during this time.

Dr. Hammond also suggests setting aside regular periods for heart-to-heart conversations with your kids. Let them know they can freely share any feelings they are having, and validate the feelings they share.

2. Find creative ways to get moving.

The darker, colder winter months don't provide as much opportunity for outdoor activity and movement. But physical activity is extremely important for your and your kids' mental health. Make it a goal to ensure the whole family gets some form of exercise every day.

"You are the role model for your kids right now, more than ever," Dr. Schlesinger says. She suggests trying yoga, exercise videos or some fun games that incorporate movement with your kids.

3. Rely on routines.

Kids feel calmest when their lives are predictable, so it's no surprise that the unpredictable nature of living through a pandemic causes stress for them. That makes the routines you can control even more important. Set predictable meal times (and try to eat with your kids as much as possible so you can connect with them), stick to consistent bedtime routines and make sure your kids are going to bed at the same time every night.

4. Give kids some control.

Like most adults, kids just want to feel like they have control. You can give them a sense of control (and calm) by letting them choose, for example, whether to wear jeans or sweatpants, whether to have pasta or chicken for dinner, or whether they want to watch their TV show before or after lunch.

"With so many changes outside of children's control, it is imperative that they start to feel emotionally safe again in their environment and have some positive sense of control," advises Dr. Hammond.

5. Take care of your own mental health.

There's a reason the flight attendant tells you to put your oxygen mask on before you put one on your child. You have to take care of yourself so you can take care of others, and that's true for your mental health as well.

Dr. Schlesinger says parents should set aside time for themselves away from their kids—to exercise, watch TV, read or engage in other activities they enjoy. Doing so shows your kids that it's important to prioritize one's own needs so they are better equipped to take care of their needs now and in the future.

It's also vital for each parent to confide in a support person regularly, whether it's your spouse, a friend or a therapist.

6. Get professional help.

If your child is exhibiting concerning behaviors that you aren't able to fully address at home, it's time to reach out for help. Your pediatrician's office can recommend pediatric psychiatrists and psychologists who are equipped to help you and your child.

Dr. Schlesinger notes that kids who had known behavioral health concerns prior to the pandemic—such as anxiety, or those who experienced a trauma they had dealt with—have a lower threshold for seeking professional help now.

For kids that didn't have pre-existing behavioral health issues, if their behavior has changed substantially and you aren't able to help them get to a place of happiness, or if they begin to exhibit aggressive behaviors, it's time to seek professional help.

WORKING MOMS HAVE HAD ENOUGH OF LEARNING AND TEACHING RESILIENCE

I don't need more lessons—for myself or my kids—after rising above all that the pandemic has thrown at us.

by Mita Mallick

"NOOOOOOOOOOOOOOOOOOOOOOOOOOOOOO."

I came dashing up the stairs, in a panic.

"Is everything OK? What happened? Who's hurt?"

"She lost at UNO Trolls," my husband said, shrugging his shoulders. He packed the cards away and walked around her. "It's time for bed now."

And there was our 5-year-old, rolling around on the ground, not just crying, but wailing at the top of her lungs, because Daddy had just beaten her at UNO.

"Why didn't you let her win?"

"Why would I let her win?"

"Why not?"

Of our many pandemic parenting struggles, whether to teach our kids resilience when it comes to losing is the debate we can't move past.

"You can't always let them win," my husband lectures me. "They need to learn how to lose. They need to be resilient."

I would argue that our kids are nothing but resilient now. Wearing masks every day to school. Playing with only each other at home. Mastering logging in and out of Zoom links for classes and activities. Missing seeing our extended family regularly. Coping with summer 2020 being canceled. And coming to terms with Halloween 2020 being canceled as well.

What else could UNO Trolls teach them? Haven't they learned enough resilience? I certainly have.

I am tired of learning resilience in our new world of remote working in a pandemic. Budget cuts at work. De-prioritization. Re-prioritization. Surviving all day meetings on Zoom. Moving from my makeshift desk to the couch to the kitchen table back to the makeshift desk again. Working, teaching, cooking, working, cleaning, parenting, screaming and working some more. I'm all set with resiliency for now. I have had enough resilience for 2020. Come back again and visit me next year, please.

I suspect this is how my husband secretly feels as well. He's tired of being resilient. So he wants to win at UNO Trolls every single time.

UNO Trolls. Junior Scrabble. Operation. Connect 4. Candy Land. Chutes and Ladders. Stacks of board games to bond over and to pass the time during this pandemic. Somehow, no matter how many other games we tried to play, all roads lead back to UNO Trolls. And of course, the happy bonding only occurs when I lose, and they win shouting, "UNO OUT!"

According to the American Psychological Association's resilience guide for parents and teachers, as children build resilience, they will experience difficulty and distress. Hence the seven minutes of wailing and rolling around the ground after my husband served our daughter the "+4" card.

Out of the APA's 10 tips for building resiliency, I found these to be most useful:

- "Help your child by helping them help others" I thought was interesting, until I realized that asking my son to help my daughter only ensued in another wrestling, punching and biting match.
- The "maintain a daily routine" is just another reminder of the schedule/routine shaming I feel barraged by; the only thing I can be certain of is that they will eat breakfast, lunch and dinner, fight with each other, cry over losing UNO Trolls, and maybe take a shower.
- And the final tip on "Keep things in perspective and maintain a positive outlook" I suppose hasn't worked well for me, as we start the UNO Trolls game and I shout, "Take whatever card you want and let's get this over with!"

The tips that I did find helpful for building resilience around UNO Trolls started with "Take a break." OK, so we don't need to play six rounds in a row. Maybe they take a break and watch some Peppa Pig, while I pass out on the couch for a solid five minutes. Or how about "Move toward your goals," which means how about we stop playing UNO Trolls and move onto Operation or another board game? And finally "Accept change" when on three occasions, I had successfully hidden UNO Trolls, forcing them to engage in a different activity, after they spent a solid 11 minutes looking for the cards, while I was able to mindlessly scroll on my phone.

Enough with resilience, I say. Let them win. It's OK. I have learned enough resilience in the past 30 weeks. We all have. I just want to finish this game of UNO Trolls, get them to bed, so I can sit on the couch eating Reese's Pieces and pass out watching another thrilling episode of *90 Day Fiancé*.

Mita Mallick is the Head of Diversity and Cross Cultural Marketing for Unilever North America and loves living in Jersey City with her husband and two young kiddos.

VP MOM TO CRITICS: 'I AM VERY PROUD OF LOOKING TIRED'

We love her take on our biggest pet peeve.
by Quinn Fish

The next time you're thinking of telling a working mom—or *anyone* for that matter—they look tired, we suggest you just don't. One mom, fortunately, had the best response on LinkedIn when someone messaged her to tell her how she looked.

Melanie Borden, a mom of girls ages 5 and 7 and the VP of Marketing at a New York City–based car company, explained that after posting a recent video to LinkedIn, someone deemed it necessary to tell her she looked tired. *And who doesn't?*

Her post detailed how every working mom is doing the best she can, and it's a must-read:

> *Yes I am tired. On behalf of everyone everywhere worldwide we are all tired from 2020.*
> *Especially working parents.*
> *Outside of work I am a mom. My kids are my No. 1 priority and now we are doing virtual school again for the second time around this year.*

Plus the normal parent things outside of a global pandemic like being woken up at night, sick kids, etc.

I am very proud of looking tired, I work my tail off as both a mom and employee.

If looking tired is a badge of honor for my accomplishments this year, I'll take it!!

Amen, Mama. Melanie's raw honesty in how she's juggling her responsibilities as a mom and an employee is inspiring to us all—and by the way, if she looks tired, we're not sure what that means for us. This year has been utter chaos and everyone deserves a little bit of slack.

You know what else we're tired of? People judging working parents for not having everything together all the time—especially in the COVID era. Melanie, who looks like a stellar working mom to us, is setting an example for her little ones that it's OK for family to come first, regardless of other responsibilities.

"[This year] has been so challenging for everyone, but as working moms, it's especially hard for us," Melanie told *Working Mother*. "We are the hardest on ourselves, and each other. We judge ourselves for everything from how we look to how we parent. We have been tasked with an extra challenge of navigating through this year while teaching, working, parenting and trying to retain some sense of ourselves. [In 2020], I have learned to be kind to myself and that my children need the stability and structure, and their well-being is my priority."

She isn't the only mom to showcase her realness on LinkedIn during this crisis. A few months ago, one consultant mom explained why she switched her profile picture from a "glossy" headshot to one that showcases her true reality. Another mom admitted she's "not sorry" for being a working mom—inspiring us to be wholeheartedly unapologetic about our priorities.

If there's one silver lining of the pandemic, it's this: Working moms can finally be shamelessly transparent about everything that's on our plates. Our colleagues can actually see—in Zooms and otherwise—everything we're dealing with. So there's no longer an excuse for us not to get the flexibility and support we deserve.

10 SURVIVAL STRATEGIES FOR A LONG WINTER OF DISTANCE LEARNING AND WORKING FROM HOME

Experts and real working moms share realistic strategies that will help keep us all sane through the chilly months.

by Gia Miller

Most of us have already experienced what it's like to be working from home while our children are trapped indoors all day—and it hasn't been pretty. Here's how to get through a long winter.

1. Take a deep breath. Actually, take several—and do it often.
Right now, soften and relax your belly, then take a deep breath in through your nose and out through your mouth. Then do it again. It's simple and extremely effective. Deep breathing is the first step to managing your stress and creating balance. Plus, you can do it with your kids.

"If you set aside three or four minutes, three or four times a day to practice what I call 'soft belly breathing,' it will balance your fight or flight stress response and allow you to come back into balance," says James S. Gordon, M.D., founder and executive director of the

Center for Mind-Body Medicine and author of *The Transformation: Discovering Wholeness and Healing After Trauma*. "When you make this a daily practice, it will change the structure of your brain. Research has shown that regular concentrated or mindfulness meditation can decrease the size of the amygdala, which is the center of fear and anger."

2. Shake it up! Your body, that is.

Exercise is an important way to help decrease your anxiety, stress and irritability. Both you *and* your kids need regular movement to get through this stressful period, even when it's cold outside. Bundle up and go for a walk or plan an activity in the snow.

"One of my favorite techniques is shaking and dancing. You shake for five or six minutes to fast, rhythmic music, pause for a couple of minutes and then let your body move to music that's energizing and inspiring," says Gordon. "It changes the whole vicious cycle of anxiety, irritability, fearfulness and anger and helps bring you back into physiological balance."

3. Throw a tantrum!

If you're really frustrated or overwhelmed, you have Gordon's permission to throw a fit!

"Go into a quiet room and put a sign on the door that reads, 'Mommy is freaking out for 10 minutes,' then scream and shout, throw pillows, jump up and down or even cry," he advises. "Do whatever you need to do to get it out. Then, all of your other tools and techniques will work. It's not a time for therapy. It's not a time for good wishes or positive affirmations. It's a time to get it out of your system."

Cindy Graham, Ph.D., licensed psychologist and founder-owner of Brighter Hope Wellness Center stresses that while it's important to allow yourself the opportunity to release your frustration, remember that it's key for kids to see or hear how you manage your emotions in those moments. So don't do (or say!) anything you wouldn't want them to.

4. Let them have their tantrums, too.
Our culture teaches us to be very stoic, but Gordon believes that's a deep misunderstanding of human nature.

"It's an imposition and a social value that's really destructive," he says. "If your kid is throwing a tantrum at home, take a step back and let them have their tantrum for as long they want. Just be nearby to make sure no one gets hurt and nothing is destroyed. You can also try to prevent the tantrum by noticing when they're getting anxious, bored or restless. Start by moving around—dance with them, jump up and down, or go outside for a couple minutes."

5. Cut yourself, and your kids, some slack.
Seriously, make it easier on yourself. No one is perfect, and this is not the time to strive for the Mother of the Year award. Pick your battles strategically and don't fight over the small stuff. Create a structure that makes sense for your family, and let them have some extra screen time if it means you can get your work done in peace.

"My motto is 'good is good enough and sometimes bad is also good enough,'" says Allison Boudreau, an artist mom of four in New York City. "You have to keep things in perspective and look at the big picture. Eventually, this is all going to end, and we'll figure out the rest then. We should embrace where we're at and not pretend things are the same as they were before. Do what you can right now, lower your expectations and focus on surviving, not thriving."

6. Share the burden and ask for help.
It's hard to do this alone, so find help wherever you can. If you have a partner or spouse, divide the responsibilities so the childcare

burden doesn't fall fully on your shoulders. If it's all too unmanageable, arrange a meeting with your children's teachers to ask for help. Explain that you won't be able to check that they've logged into each class or completed classwork and that you'll need additional support.

The same thing goes with your boss. Most employers recognize how difficult this time is, so ask for more breaks throughout the day or flexibility in your schedule. It'll allow you to be more available to help your kids and give you more opportunities to take time for yourself when needed.

7. Reward good behavior.

Find what motivates your child—money, toys, screen time, etc.— and offer it as a reward for good behavior. Rewarding the good, instead of punishing the bad, will help them build new, positive habits.

"In March, I opened a 'store' in our house," explains Cassandra Maughan, a mom of three in Kansas and registered nurse. "I bought play money and they earn a dollar a day for good behavior. If they aren't on task or give me a hard time with school, they lose the dollar for that day. On Friday, after school has ended, they go 'shopping' with whatever they've earned. The store is just a tote bag filled with little toys, candy, hair supplies, makeup, etc., but they're always excited. I don't know if they'll let me close it once the pandemic ends!"

8. Schedule family time.

"You aren't the only one trapped in this mess—the entire family is as well," says Renee Harris, a Georgia mom of two and the director of development and marketing for Hillels of Georgia. "We all need a change of pace once in a while, so make time to do fun family activities together. Take a walk, play a game, watch a movie or cook your favorite meal. Everyone's stress is heightened when work and school occur in the same house. It's important to still have fun together so those stressful moments aren't as tense."

According to Graham, daily family time helps our kids feel secure. Try to spend time with your kids in the morning with something simple like singing a song or eating breakfast together. When you check in with them and give them hugs, it'll satisfy their need for attention so they can confidently do things on their own while you work.

9. Manage expectations and create new opportunities.

If you're worried about the holiday break this year, begin by talking to your children and validating their feelings.

"Explain what this break will look like because kids tend to be very focused on what's happening at the moment and they don't have the perspective to understand why these changes need to occur," says Gordon. "Encourage them to tell you how they feel about it, and listen to their concerns, whatever they are."

Once you've managed their expectations, Graham suggests creating schedules to keep kids in a routine, encouraging creativity and new passions, and scheduling "Zoom babysitting" calls with family members you won't be able to see this holiday season.

10. Look on the bright side.

Yes, there *is* a bright side to all of this. According to Gordon, if you use these skills, along with any others that work for you, you can come out of this with a greater understanding of how to deal with challenges of any kind.

"For the last 30 years, I've intensively worked with people who suffered trauma due to war, climate-related disasters and school shootings," he says. "Once they learn some basic skills and tools to come into balance, their imagination and intuition are a little freer. If you implement this now, then you can come out of this situation more whole, more resilient, and even healthier than you were before. Your mood will change and your sense of your own abilities and capacity will change. Everyone should know this is a real possibility for them."

THIS MILITARY MOM'S 'GRIT' EXERCISE IS KEY TO SURVIVING THE PANDEMIC

The lessons she learned during deployment can help every mom stay sane right now.

by Shannon Huffman Polson

Working moms all over the US are bearing the brunt of guiding kids through educational challenges, whether it be distance learning or partially in-person schooling—on top of working full-time. Forced to navigate the new professional terrain of remote work under tumultuous conditions with no certain outcome, it's no exaggeration to say this is a challenge unlike any we've ever faced.

As one of the first women to fly the Apache helicopter in the US Army with service on three continents, I'm no stranger to challenges. But as a mother of two boys, the pandemic has thrown me back on my heels, too.

I flew helicopters long before I had children, and it is frankly much simpler to only be thinking of yourself. Even leading teams in both the military and the corporate world, those teams are working together in the face of challenge. The responsibility of raising and educating little humans—who are wildly more resilient than we give them credit for—is a very different beast.

Over the last few years, I've interviewed dozens of women leaders in the military, pioneering women general officers, a submariner, a combat rescue swimmer, and one of the first women Army Rangers for my book, *The Grit Factor.* I asked them, what gave them their grit? What had given me MY grit back then? And, perhaps most importantly, in the face of today's challenges, how can connecting to and developing grit get us through such a complicated time?

A growth mindset, one that values the learning and growth that come from challenges, is a critical starting place. One aspect of the mindset that will support your success in difficult times is *grounded optimism.* The women leaders I spoke with were deliberate about putting aside the sense of overwhelm and deciding instead to see *what they could learn* from the challenges they faced—with utter faith in the outcome. Their ability to reframe challenges into opportunities was a key factor of their success. The science is clear that those who go into a challenge knowing it can make them better in fact come out ahead, performing better on many measures of success.

There's a reframing exercise which is a part of the Army's Master Resilience training program that is particularly helpful as we navigate the COVID era. The exercise is not unique to the military; it comes from the University of Pennsylvania's Positive Psychology program and decades of research supporting small but powerful steps toward navigating difficulty. The Army uses it for both soldiers and their families to mitigate the difficulties of the military's rapid deployment cadence and the challenges of reintegration. This reframing exercise asks us to add sentence starters to reconsider limiting assumptions. Here are the three sentence starters:

1. *That's not completely true because . . .*
2. *A more optimistic way of looking at this would be . . .*
3. *The most likely implication is . . .*

Pick one of your assumptions. Here's mine most recently (I'm sure more than a few of you can relate): *There is no way I can take on this homeschooling requirement on top of managing my career.*

I'd pick a sentence starter:

1. *That's not completely true because my children do not need my full attention as they are completing assignments. I will be able to find time to conduct business calls and make progress with my career.*
2. *A more optimistic way of looking at this will be that I will have a chance to be more connected to my children and their education, which I've really wanted, and if I work to manage my time well, we will all grow from this experience.*
3. *The most likely implication is that I will have to make compromises and find ways to achieve my goals while I ensure that my children are learning and growing.*

You may want to try this while thinking of a challenge you may be facing in your career, or in a recent project. Reframing is a powerful technique that forces us to own our mindset, a more amorphous concept, with a very tactical exercise. This exercise, in turn, helps us to shape what otherwise seems difficult to change, especially in the face of uncertainty and overwhelm.

What are the assumptions that are limiting your life? Try the reframing technique. One of the things I know for sure is that grit is not only for mountain climbers and military pilots—grit is innate to every single one of us. You might have to do a little work to find it, but you'll likely realize it was there all along.

Shannon Huffman Polson is founder and CEO of The Grit Institute, a leadership development organization dedicated to ethical, people-centered leadership. She is one of the first women to fly the Apache helicopter in the US Army, and a veteran of the corporate world as well. She is the author of The Grit Factor: Courage, Resilience and Leadership in the Most Male-Dominated Organization in the World *(Harvard Business Review Press, 2020). She holds her MBA from the Tuck School at Dartmouth and her MFA.*

HOW TO EMERGE FROM THE PANDEMIC AS A MENTALLY STRONGER, HAPPIER FAMILY

This year has been utter chaos. These mindset tweaks can help.

by Joy Altimare

Well, it's official. With less than nine weeks left until 2021, 2020 has been and *still is* a distinctively unique year—a year hopefully never to be repeated. A year, hopefully, that leads to only positivity and an amazing future.

As we push through the blur of repetitive days (*What's today's date?*) and unbelievable conversations (*What's hybrid learning?*), working moms all over the country are redefining and reimagining ways to keep themselves, their families and their kids productive, positive and focused on succeeding—despite the chaos that is 2020. Here are some of the tips that help me keep my kiddos (and myself!) on the right track:

I believe in the power of positive affirmation. I model it for my daughter.

Every morning, I spend a little quiet time alone, I journal a bit and I speak positivity into the day. I also have parts of my affirmation posted around the house and office. It's a great reminder throughout the day to pause, check in with myself and stay focused on things that move me toward progress. Now, my daughter has her own affirmation that she says during breakfast, and I've watched her carry that confidence when she is in the virtual classroom and things become a bit too hard on the computer. She pauses, closes her eyes, takes a deep breath and says a few positive phrases to maintain her calmness. While it doesn't work like magic—*Tada, computer fixed!*—it is a magical scene to observe. And, while she's been practicing her affirmation since she was 3 years old, this season of unpredictability has allowed her to really lean into that foundation to center herself whenever she needs to. I find it reassuring that she has a tool that, hopefully, she'll carry with her into her teenage years and adulthood.

A great schedule, organization and transparency are essential.
Since my daughter is in a virtual classroom most of the day, she must remain on a structured schedule. Thankfully, we've retained some sense of "new" normalcy, which I believe is the key to providing comfort for kiddos, by re-imagining how she'll attend her weekly extracurriculars and enrichment programs. She still has her piano, chess and Mandarin lessons in person (everyone is screened before arrival), but now she has soccer and theater, both virtually. Those extra opportunities to connect with classmates and friends around a more physical activity provide a respite from the academic rigors of the day. And, just so she doesn't panic, we have a white board with the schedule (for easy updating when things change) and I leverage technology (Alexa!) to set reminders so that she can practice a little independence rather than asking me when she needs to go to certain activities. A structured day and healthy routines (like a consistent bedtime) help create a sense of order to the day that also offers reassurance.

Although most of us are still spending most (if not all) of our time in the same home, it's really important to spend individual, one-on-one time with your children.

I call it "special time-in," and it's a great way to be present with each child to reinforce how special they are. It could be as simple as making cookies together, while you ask some questions to check in on their schoolwork and mental stamina; or maybe 15 minutes in the morning for a cup of tea (and maybe juice for the kiddo). This works for kids of all ages; individual, uninterrupted (no cell phones!) time with each of them helps everyone feel special and ready to be their best selves.

While being productive is important, it's also key to decide, today, where you want your family to be when we get on the other side of this pandemic. When this school year is over and we've figured out a way for all kiddos to be in class and we no longer have the benefit of time together, where do you want your family unit to be? Stronger together? Happy and positive? Loving and supportive? That's the focus—to emerge better than how we entered. And part of that is listening to yourself and carving out time to listen to your kiddos to create a sense of support and peace in your home.

Joy Altimare is the chief engagement and brand officer at the industry leader in health and prevention for over 100 years, EHE Health. With over 16 years of experience in the marketing field, Joy has become an expert adviser to organizations looking to tackle growth, innovation and technology challenges. Prior to joining the health care world, Joy worked on brands such as L'Oreal, Verizon and Colgate-Palmolive at such agencies as Ogilvy+Mather, GREY and Publicis.